HOW'S YOUR HEALTH?

Allergies

Angela Royston

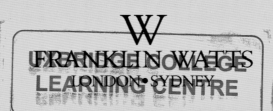
FRANKLIN WATTS
LONDON • SYDNEY

First published in 2006 by
Franklin Watts
338 Euston Road
London NW1 3BH

Franklin Watts Australia
Hachette Children's Books
Level 17/207 Kent Street
Sydney NSW 2000

Copyright © Franklin Watts 2006

Produced by Calcium, New Brook House, 385 Alfreton Road, Nottingham, NG7 5LR

Editor: Sarah Eason
Design: Paul Myerscough
Illustration: Annie Boberg and Geoff Ward
Picture research: Sarah Jameson
Consultant: Dr Stephen Earwicker

Acknowledgements:
The publisher would like to thank the following for permission to reproduce photographs:
Alamy p.14, p.22, p.23, p.25, p.27; Istockphoto p.8; Corbis p.15; OSF p.24; Getty p.6; Tudor
Photography p.7, p.10, p.12, p.21; Chris Fairclough Photography p.9, p.11, p.16, p.17, p.18,
p.20, p.26.

Every attempt has been made to clear copyright. Should there be any inadvertent omission
please apply to the publisher for rectification.

A CIP catalogue record for this book is available from the British Library.

Dewey Decimal Classification Number: 616.97

ISBN-10: 0 7496 6674 9
ISBN-13: 978 0 7496 6674 3

Printed in China

Contents

What is an allergy?

An allergy makes your body react to something as if it is harmful, although it is not harmful to most people.

People can be **allergic** to different things. Some people are allergic to certain foods, such as strawberries or peanuts. These are healthy foods that most people enjoy, but people who are allergic to them will be ill if they eat them.

Some people are allergic to things they touch.
Other people are allergic to things they breathe
in, such as **pollen**. Pollen is a fine dust that is
made in spring and summer by grass, trees and
flowers. People with **hayfever** are allergic to pollen.
Hayfever makes your eyes sore and your nose run.

Who has allergies?

Anyone can have an allergy, but allergies usually run in families. You cannot catch an allergy.

People are more likely to have an allergy if one of their parents is allergic to something. This does not always mean that they will be allergic to the same thing. One of these girls is allergic to chocolate, but her mother is allergic to pollen.

For much of the time, most people with an allergy live like everyone else.

How you can help:

+ If you have an allergy, stay away from the thing you are allergic to.
+ If someone else has an allergy, keep them away from anything that makes them allergic.

9

What is a food allergy?

If someone has a food allergy they will be ill if they eat the food that they are allergic to.

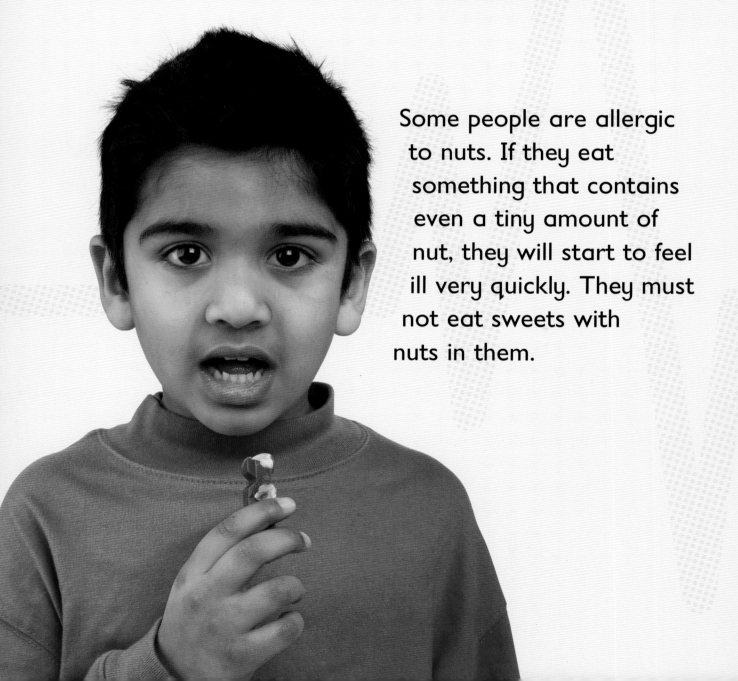

Some people are allergic to nuts. If they eat something that contains even a tiny amount of nut, they will start to feel ill very quickly. They must not eat sweets with nuts in them.

Some foods that people are allergic to:

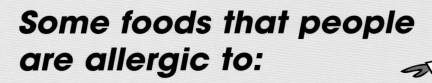

+ Peanuts and other kinds of nuts.
+ Eggs.
+ Milk, cheese, yoghurt and other foods made of milk.
+ **Seafood**, such as shrimps, prawns and mussels.
+ **Soya beans**.
+ Things made from **wheat**, such as bread, pasta, cakes and biscuits.

People with a nut allergy may be very sick if they eat nuts. They will continue to feel ill until their body has got rid of all the nuts they have eaten.

How do food allergies affect people?

A food allergy can affect someone's mouth, stomach, **intestines** and even their skin.

If somone eats something they are allergic to, their mouth and throat may swell up and go **numb**. The person may be sick and have **diarrhoea**.

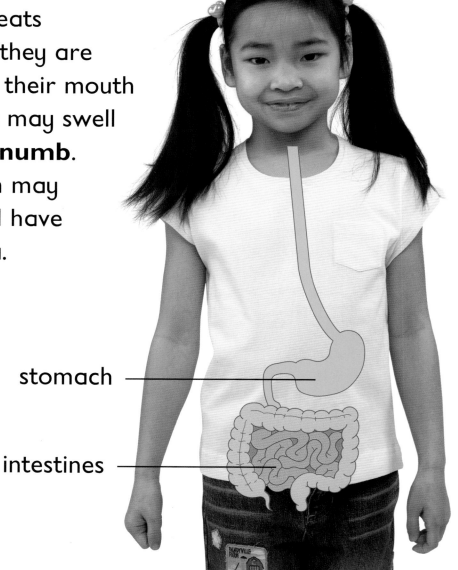

stomach

intestines

A food allergy can also affect other parts of the body. A person's skin may go red and become itchy. Their nose may run and they may sneeze a lot. They may also feel dizzy.

How you can help:

+ If the allergy does not make you too ill, rest until you feel better.
+ Keep calm.
+ If someone else is affected by a food allergy, keep them calm.
+ If the person is very ill, ask an adult to call an ambulance at once.

What is a breathing allergy?

A breathing allergy makes you sneeze and your nose run. It is like having a cold.

People who have a breathing allergy are allergic to something they breathe in, such as cigarette smoke. It can affect their lungs and eyes as well as their nose. They may cough and their eyes may become itchy and swollen.

Some things that cause a breathing allergy:

+ **Dust mites**.
+ Dust from pet fur and bird feathers.
+ Cigarette smoke.
+ **Mould**.
+ Pollen.

A breathing allergy can be treated by using a special spray. The spray contains a medicine called **antihistamine**. It stops the body being affected by the allergy. Never use an antihistamine spray if you do not have a breathing allergy.

What is a skin allergy?

A skin allergy makes a person's skin sore, red or itchy when they touch the thing they are allergic to.

Washing powders clean your clothes, but some people are allergic to the **chemicals** in them. **Biological washing powders** have special chemicals that many people are allergic to.

Bio
Washing powder

If you have a skin allergy, don't scratch the itch – this will only make it worse. People with **eczema** have patches of very dry, itchy skin. Eczema is often made worse by skin and food allergies.

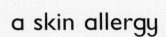

a skin allergy

Things that often cause skin allergies:

+ Insect bites.
+ **Cosmetics**.
+ Scented soaps.
+ Biological washing powders.
+ Household cleaners, such as floor cleaners and bath cleaners.

How are skin allergies treated?

Special creams help to soothe skin allergies and stop them itching.

Different creams can help to stop skin itching and feeling sore. They do not stop the allergy itself, but they can make your skin feel better.

The best way for people to treat a skin allergy is to stay away from the things that they are allergic to. People with skin allergies can buy **non-biological washing powder**, pure soap and cosmetics that do not affect their skin.

How you can help:

+ Use a cream as soon as your skin becomes sore or itchy.
+ Don't use cosmetics or washing powders that affect your skin.
+ Stay away from things you are allergic to.

What is extreme shock?

Extreme shock is when a person's whole body suddenly reacts very badly to something.

A wasp sting hurts most people and makes a small red mark on their skin. A wasp sting can also cause extreme shock in some people if they are allergic to it. Other things, such as seafood or medicines, can also cause extreme shock.

Symptoms of extreme shock:

+ **Wheezing** or difficulty in breathing.
+ Coughing.
+ Sickness, diarrhoea and stomach ache.
+ Heart beating much faster than usual.
+ Skin turning red or blue.
+ Not being able to think or talk clearly.
+ Fainting.

Find out what to do if someone has extreme shock on page 22.

When someone suffers from extreme shock, they may find it difficult to breathe. They may also have stomach ache and be sick. The person is affected almost at once.

21

How is extreme shock treated?

If a person has extreme shock, they must take a special medicine straight away.

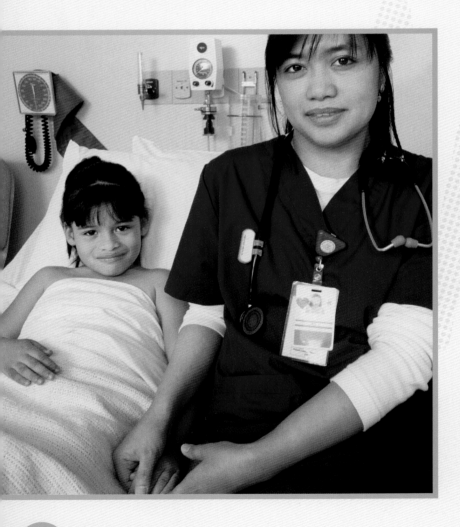

If someone suffers from extreme shock, they need to be treated by a doctor very quickly. An ambulance should be called at once.

Two medicines are used to treat extreme shock. One is **injected** to help the heart to beat normally. The second medicine is an antihistamine tablet, which people chew to stop their body reacting badly to the allergy.

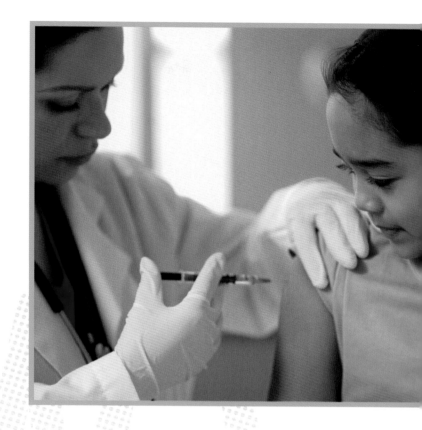

Take care!

Extreme shock medicines are very strong and must *never* be taken by anyone else. People who know they can suffer from extreme shock should carry special medicine with them. They should also wear a necklace or bracelet that will tell the doctor about their allergy.

Is there a test for allergies?

Hospitals can test people to see what they are allergic to.

Sometimes people do not know what they are allergic to. In an allergy **clinic** a nurse puts a small amount of different things a person might be allergic to into their skin.

If someone is allergic to something in the allergy test, it will make their skin go red.

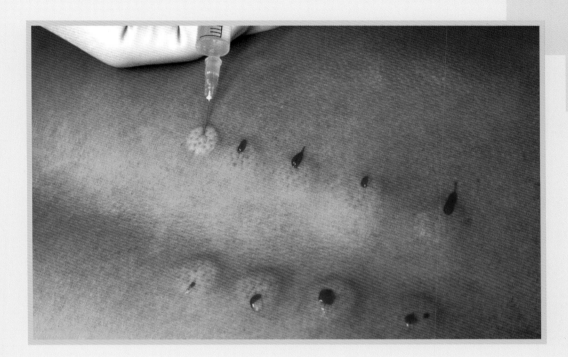

Some allergies can be shown by a **blood test**.

Other tests

Another way in which people can find out what they are allergic to is by staying away from all the things that might be causing their allergy. When they start to use each of these things again, one at a time, they should be able to tell which one causes the allergy.

Do allergies get better?

Many children have allergies that get better as they grow older.

Children often grow out of allergies. This boy is allergic to cats. Many children are allergic to certain foods, such as cheese.

By the time people become adults, they may no longer be allergic. This woman was allergic to pet hair when she was a child. Now she is an adult, she is no longer allergic. However, many old people become allergic to things that did not affect them before.

Glossary

allergic   to have an allergy.

antihistamine   medicine that stops the body reacting to something it is allergic to.

biological washing powder   washing powder that contains chemicals called enzymes.

blood test   when a small amount of blood is taken from someone to find out things about their body.

chemical   powerful substance found in many man-made things, including cleaning and beauty products.

clinic   place where people are treated by doctors and nurses.

cosmetics   creams and make-up that people put on their skin.

diarrhoea   when the solid waste your body makes (your poo) is loose and runny.

dust mite   tiny spider-like animal that lives in house dust.

eczema   condition that makes the skin dry and itchy.

hayfever   allergy to pollen.

inject   the way in which liquid medicine is put into the body through a needle.

intestine   part of the body that deals with food and waste.

mould   furry coat that grows on old food or damp things.

non-biological washing powder   washing powder that does not contain chemicals called enzymes.

numb   without feeling.

pollen   fine yellow dust made by flowers, grass and some trees in spring and early summer.

seafood   sea animals that can be eaten, such as prawns, shrimps and mussels.

soya bean   bean that can be made into different foods, such as milk and yoghurt.

wheat   crop that is made into food, such as bread, cakes and biscuits.

wheeze   sound that people make when they are finding it difficult to breathe.

Find out more

Find out all about allergies:
www.bbc.co.uk/health/conditions/allergies/

Read about allergies on Allergy UK's website:
www.allergyuk.org

Every effort has been made by the Publisher to ensure that these websites contain no inappropriate or offensive material. However, because of the nature of the Internet, it is impossible to guarantee that the contents of these sites will not be altered. We strongly advise that Internet access is supervised by a responsible adult.

Index